PLAY ACTION

Grow a bilingual vocabulary by:

- **Looking** at pictures and words
- **Talking** about what you see
- **Touching** and naming objects
- **Using** questions to extend learning...
  Ask questions that invite children
  to share information.
  Begin your questions with words like...
  who, what, when, where and how.

Desarrolle su vocabulario bilingüe:

- **Mire** los dibujos y las palabras
- **Hable** de lo que ves
- **Toque** y nombre objetos
- **Use** preguntas para aumentar el aprendizaje...
  Use preguntas que invitan a
  los niños a compartir la información.
  Empiece sus frases con el uso de estas palabras...
  ¿quién? ¿qué? ¿cuándo? ¿por dónde? y ¿cómo?

Learning Props, L.L.C.

JUEGO EN ACCIÓN

I can...
Yo puedo...

swim
nadar

crawl
gatear

run
correr

gallop
galopar

jump
saltar

dance
bailar

swing
columpiarse

hop
brincar

balance
balancearse

I can...
Yo puedo...

fish
pescar

climb
trepar/subir

roll
revolcarme

cheer
vitorear/celebrar

tiptoe
caminar de puntillas

clap
aplaudir

sled
montar en trineo

I can...
Yo puedo...

tie
a shoe

atar
el zapato/
amarrar
el zapato

build
construir

do puzzles
resolver
los rompecabezas

color
colorear

paint
pintar

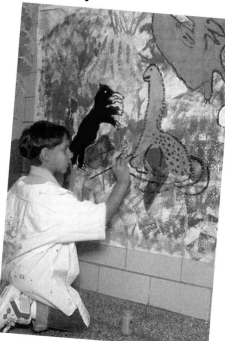

read
leer

write
escribir

I can...
Yo puedo...

ride a bike
montar en bicicleta

make a face
hacer una mueca

hug
abrazar

kiss
besar

I can...
Yo puedo...

blow bubbles
soplar burbujas / hacer burbujas

take a picture
tomar una foto

I can eat...
Yo puedo comer...

dinner
la cena

a cracker
una galleta

watermelon
la sandía

with a spoon
con la cuchara

an apple
una manzana

a lollipop
una paleta

a banana
un banano

I can make music!
¡Yo puedo tocar música!

guitar
la guitarra

cello
el violoncelo

piano
el piano

keyboard
el teclado

drums
los tambores

I can march and sing!
¡Yo puedo marchar y cantar!

I can play...
Yo puedo jugar...

hopscotch
la rayuela/el tejo

games
los juegos

with a ball
con la pelota

soccer
al fútbol/al balón pie

baseball
**al béisbol/
a la pelota caliente**

with toys
con los juguetes

basketball
al baloncesto

I can pretend!
¡Yo puedo imaginar! / ¡Yo puedo actuar!

I can play with others.
Yo puedo jugar con otros/otras.

I can play alone.
Yo puedo jugar solo/sola.

pronunciation

I can/**eye kan**	Yo puedo/**Yo pway**-doh
crawl/**krawl**	gatear/gah-tay-**ahr**
swim/**swim**	nadar/na-**dar**
run/**ruhn**	correr/kohr-**rair**
jump/**juhmp**	saltar/sal-**tar**
gallop/**gal**-uhp	galopar/gah-lo-**pahr**
dance/**danss**	bailar/buy-**lar**
swing/**swing**	columpiarse/khol-loom-pee-**ahr**-say
balance/**bal**-uhnss	balancearse/bah-lahn-say-**ahr**-say
hop/**hop**	brincar/breen-**car**
fish/**fish**	pescar/pace-**car**
climb/**klime**	trepar, subir/tray-**pahr**, soo-**beer**
roll/**rohl**	revolcarme/ray-vol-**car**-may
cheer/**chihr**	vitorear, celebrar/vee-tore-ay-**ahr**, sale-lay-**brahr**
tiptoe/**tip-toe**	caminar de puntillas/kah-mee-**nahr** day poon-**tee**-yahs
clap/**klap**	aplaudir/ah-plaw-**deer**
sled/**sled**	montar en trineo/moan-**tahr** ehn tree-**nay**-oh
tie a shoe/**tye uh shoo**	atar el zapato, amarrar el zapato/ah-**tahr** ehl ssah-**pah**-toe, ah-mahr-**rahr** ehl ssah-**pah**-toe
build/**bild**	construir/cones-troo-**eer**
do puzzles/**doo puhz**-uhls	resolver los rompecabezas/ray-sole-**vehr** loase rome-pay-kah-**bay**-sahs
color/**kuhl**-ur	colorear/koh-lore-ray-**ahr**
paint/**paynt**	pintar/peen-**tahr**
write/**rite**	escribir/ess-kree-**beer**
read/**reed**	leer/lay-**air**
ride a bike/**ride uh bike**	montar en bicicleta/moan-**tahr** ehn bee-see-**clay**-tah
make a face/**make uh fayss**	hacer una mueca/ahs-**air** oon-ah moo-**way**-kah
hug/**huhg**	abrazar/ah-brah-**ssahr**
kiss/**kiss**	besar/**bay**-sahr
blow bubbles/**bloh** buh-**buhls**	soplar burbujas, hacer burbujas/ soap-**lahr** boo-r-**boo**-hahs, ahs-**air** boo-r-**boo**-hahs
take a picture/**tayk uh pik**-chur	tomar una foto/toe-**mahr** oon-ah **foe**-toe